Torque brims with excitement perfect for thrill-seekers of all kinds. Discover daring survival skills, explore uncharted worlds, and marvel at mighty engines and extreme sports. In *Torque* books, anything can happen. Are you ready?

This edition first published in 2026 by Bellwether Media, Inc.

No part of this publication may be reproduced in whole or in part without written permission of the publisher. For information regarding permission, write to Bellwether Media, Inc., Attention: Permissions Department, 3500 American Blvd W, Suite 150, Bloomington, MN 55431.

Library of Congress Cataloging-in-Publication Data

Names: Birdoff, Ariel Factor, author.
Title: Dua Lipa / by Ariel Factor Birdoff.
Description: Minneapolis, MN : Bellwether Media, 2026. | Series: Music superstars | Includes bibliographical references and index. | Audience: Ages 7-12 | Audience: Grades 4-6 | Summary: "Engaging images accompany information about Dua Lipa. The combination of high-interest subject matter and light text is intended for students in grades 3 through 7"- Provided by publisher.
Identifiers: LCCN 2025001556 (print) | LCCN 2025001557 (ebook) | ISBN 9798893045000 (library binding) | ISBN 9798893046380 (ebook)
Subjects: LCSH: Lipa, Dua, 1995–Juvenile literature. | Singers–Biography–Juvenile literature. | LCGFT: Biographies.
Classification: LCC ML3930.L563 B57 2026 (print) | LCC ML3930.L563 (ebook) | DDC 782.42164092 [B]–dc23/eng/20250115
LC record available at https://lccn.loc.gov/2025001556
LC ebook record available at https://lccn.loc.gov/2025001557

Text copyright © 2026 by Bellwether Media, Inc. TORQUE and associated logos are trademarks and/or registered trademarks of Bellwether Media, Inc. Bellwether Media is a division of FlutterBee Education Group.

Editor: Rachael Barnes   Designer: Josh Brink

Printed in the United States of America, North Mankato, MN.

TABLE OF CONTENTS

At the Festival	4
Who Is Dua Lipa?	6
A Musical Dream	8
New Rules, New Artist	12
Dua Lipa's Loves	20
Glossary	22
To Learn More	23
Index	24

AT THE FESTIVAL

Colorful lights shine. Banners wave. Dua Lipa's dreams come true as she takes the stage. She is **headlining** the Glastonbury Festival in 2024!

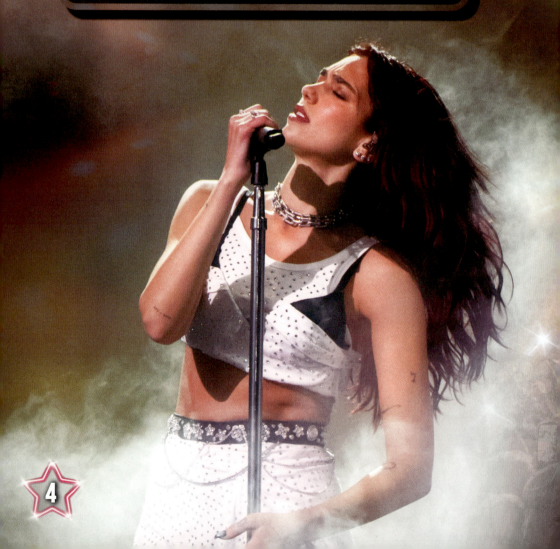

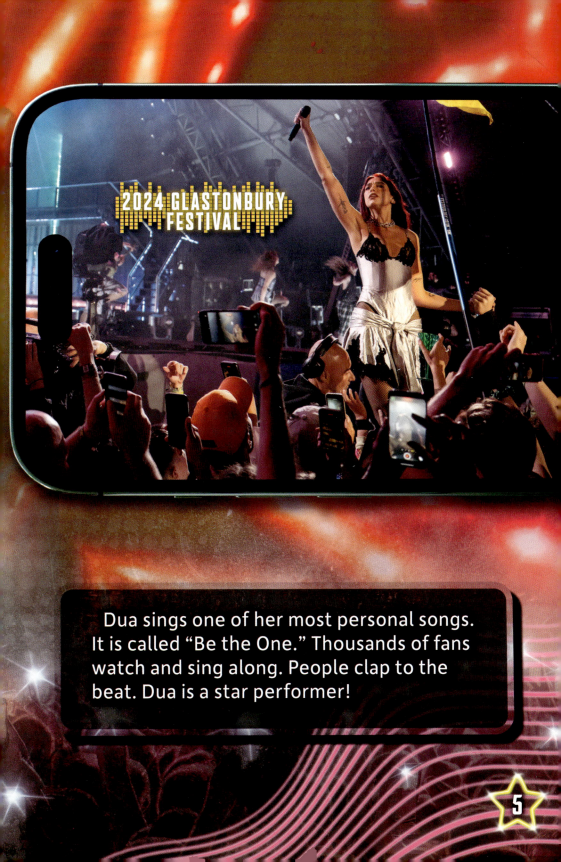

Dua sings one of her most personal songs. It is called "Be the One." Thousands of fans watch and sing along. People clap to the beat. Dua is a star performer!

WHO IS DUA LIPA?

Dua Lipa is a British-Albanian singer. She is best known for her catchy pop music. People love to dance to Dua's popular songs.

DUA LIPA

 Birthday
August 22, 1995

 Hometown
London, England

 Types of Music
pop, dance

 First Solo Hit
"New Love"

  She has won a lot of awards and has performed all over the world. She is also a successful businesswoman. She started Radical22, a company that helps Dua control her music!

A MUSICAL DREAM

Dua comes from a family of five. Her parents were **refugees** from Kosovo. They moved to London, England, where Dua and her two siblings were born.

DUA WITH HER FAMILY

WHAT IS IN A NAME?

Dua means "love" in Albanian.

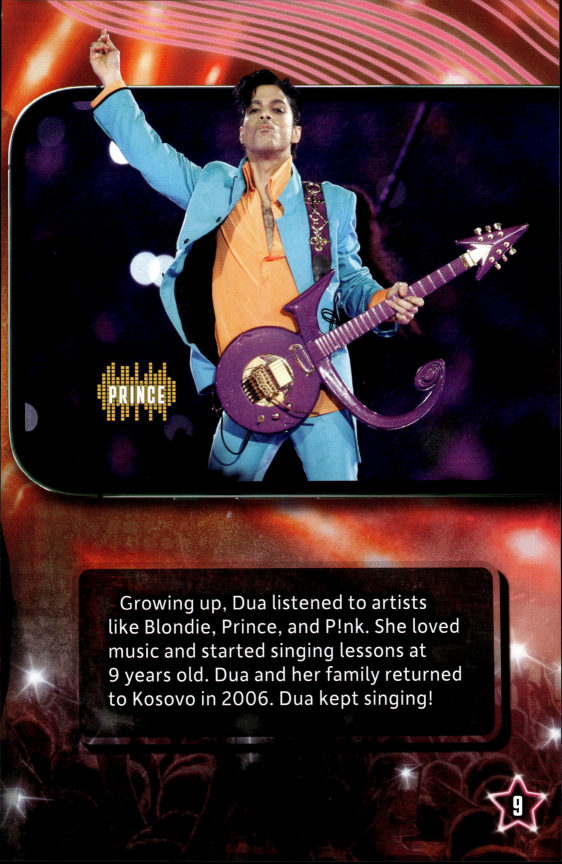

Growing up, Dua listened to artists like Blondie, Prince, and P!nk. She loved music and started singing lessons at 9 years old. Dua and her family returned to Kosovo in 2006. Dua kept singing!

When she was 15, Dua returned to London by herself. She continued attending school, but she dreamed of becoming a pop star!

FAVORITES

1990s Trend
butterfly clips

Color
green

Movie
Notting Hill

Book
A Little Life
By Hanya Yanagihara

Dua started uploading **covers** of her favorite songs on **SoundCloud**. Soon after, she began sharing her own music. In 2014, she signed a deal with what is now known as Warner Records.

11

NEW RULES, NEW ARTIST

Dua **released** "New Love" and "Be the One" in 2015. They became well-known in Europe.

LIKE FATHER, LIKE DAUGHTER

Dua Lipa's father, Dukagjin Lipa, had his own rock band called Oda.

In 2017, she released her first album, *Dua Lipa*. The song "New Rules" reached number one on the United Kingdom charts. Two years later, she won her first **Grammy Award** for Best New Artist.

In 2020, Dua released her second album, *Future Nostalgia*. The singles "Levitating" and "Don't Start Now" made it to number two on the **Billboard** Hot 100 chart in the United States.

She went on to win the Grammy for Best Pop Vocal Album in 2021! Dua also won an award for best British album of the year at the **BRIT Awards**.

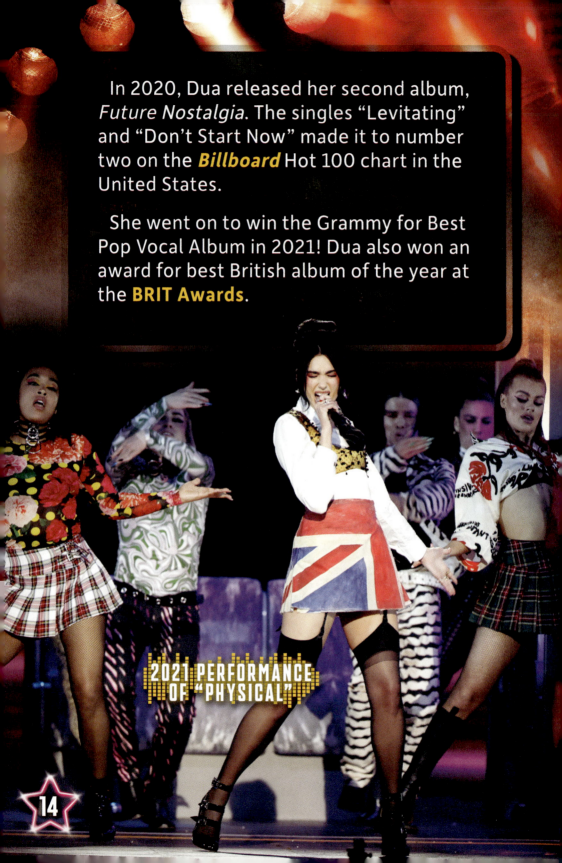

2021 PERFORMANCE OF "PHYSICAL"

AWARDS
as of February 2025

3 Grammy Awards

4 iHeartRadio Music Awards

7 BRIT Awards

1 MTV Video Music Award

2021 GRAMMY AWARDS

Dua decided to create a **livestream** concert. She **collaborated** with Elton John, Miley Cyrus, Bad Bunny, and other artists. The concert was a hit! There were more than 5 million people watching.

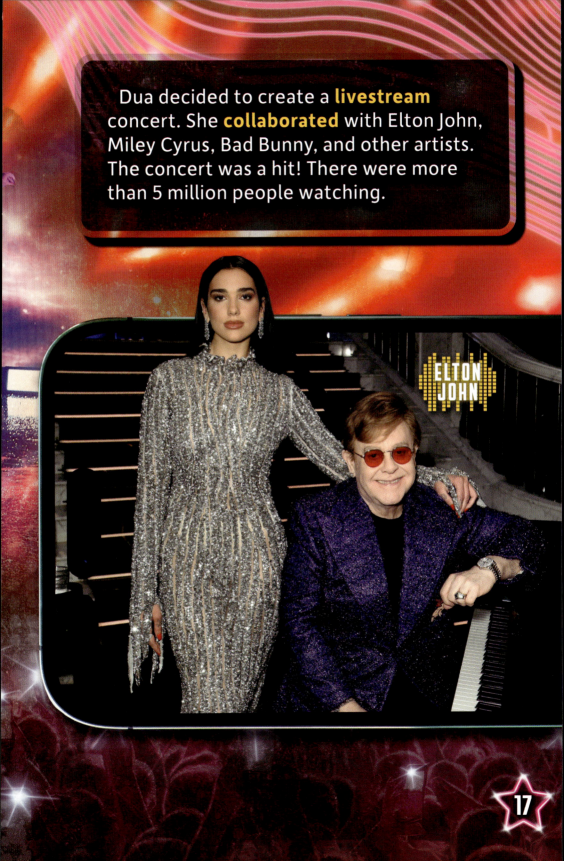

Dua's third album, *Radical Optimism*, was released in 2024. It **debuted** at number one on the U.K. Top 100 albums chart! The album encourages listeners to find the positives in tough moments.

Later that year, Dua began her Radical Optimism tour. She has performed all over the world!

MUSICAL MERMAID

Dua made her movie debut in *Barbie* in 2023. She was a mermaid Barbie!

TIMELINE

– 2014 –
Dua signs with Warner Records

– 2015 –
Dua releases her first single, "New Love"

– 2017 –
Dua releases her first album, *Dua Lipa*

— 2019 —
Dua wins her first two Grammy Awards

— 2020 —
Dua releases her second album, *Future Nostalgia*

— 2024 —
Dua releases her third album, *Radical Optimism*

19

DUA LIPA'S LOVES

When Dua goes on tour, her fans cheer her on! She calls them her loves. One of her favorite places to perform is Kosovo! Dua works with her father to run the Sunny Hill Festival. Together, they bring music to their homeland.

PLAYLIST

"New Rules"
(2017)

"Don't Start Now"
(2019)

"Levitating"
(2020)

"Dance The Night"
(2023)

"Training Season"
(2024)

Dua Lipa is living her dream. Now she hopes to bring joy to people all over the world!

21

GLOSSARY

Billboard—related to a well-known music news magazine and website that ranks songs and albums

BRIT Awards—a music awards show held in England each year; BRIT stands for British Record Industry Trusts.

collaborated—worked together to create something

coronavirus pandemic—an outbreak of the COVID-19 virus starting in December 2019 that led to millions of deaths and shutdowns around the world

covers—new performances of songs by a different singer than the original artist

debuted—was introduced or released for the first time

Grammy Award—an award given by the Recording Academy of the United States for an achievement in music; Grammy Awards are also called Grammys.

headlining—performing as the main act at a concert

livestream—related to content shared in real time for people to view online

refugees—people who leave their home for safety

released—made music available for listening

SoundCloud—a streaming platform used for uploading and listening to music, especially from new or independent artists

TO LEARN MORE

AT THE LIBRARY

Birdoff, Ariel Factor. *Bad Bunny*. Minneapolis, Minn.: Bellwether Media, 2025.

Nguyen, Suzane. *Ariana Grande*. Minneapolis, Minn.: Bellwether Media, 2025.

Richards, Mary, and David Schweitzer. *A History of Music for Children*. New York, N.Y.: Thames & Hudson, 2021.

ON THE WEB

FACTSURFER

Factsurfer.com gives you a safe, fun way to find more information.

1. Go to www.factsurfer.com.

2. Enter "Dua Lipa" into the search box and click 🔍.

3. Select your book cover to see a list of related content.

INDEX

albums, 13, 14, 18
awards, 7, 13, 14, 15
Bad Bunny, 17
Barbie, 18
Billboard, 14
Blondie, 9
childhood, 8, 9, 10, 11
coronavirus pandemic, 16
Cyrus, Miley, 17
Europe, 12
family, 8, 9, 13, 20
fans, 5, 20
favorites, 11
Glastonbury Festival, 4–5
John, Elton, 17
Kosovo, 8, 9, 20

livestream concert, 17
London, England, 8, 10
loves, 20
name, 8
P!nk, 9
playlist, 21
Prince, 9
profile, 7
Radical22, 7
songs, 5, 6, 11, 12, 13, 14, 16
SoundCloud, 11
Sunny Hill Festival, 20
timeline, 18–19
tours, 16, 18, 20
types of music, 6
Warner Records, 11

The images in this book are reproduced through the courtesy of: Joel C Ryan/ Invision/ AP/ AP Images, front cover; Catsense, front cover (light effect); Taya Ovod, pp. 2-3; Ben Houdijk, p. 3; Samir Hussein/ WireImage/ Getty Images, pp. 4, 5; Gary Miller/ Getty Images, p. 6; Karwai Tang/ WireImage/ Getty Images, p. 7; Jack Plunkett/ Invision/ AP Images, pp. 7 (VIP Pass), 18-19; David M. Benett/ Dave Benett/ Getty Images for YSL Beauty/ Getty Images, pp. 8-9; Chris O'Meara/ AP Images, p. 9; Gilles GUSTINE/ SIPA/ AP Images, p. 9; WENN/ Alamy, p. 11; OnlyZoia, p. 11 (butterfly clips); Elena11, p. 11 (paint swatch); JasonAQuest/ Wikipedia, p. 11 (*Notting Hill*); hamdi bendali, p. 11 (book); Tommy Jackson/ Getty Images, p. 12; David Jensen/ Alamy, p. 13; David M. Benett/ Dave Benett/ Getty Images, p. 14; Kevin Mazur/ Getty Images, p. 15; CarlosVdeHabsburgo/ Wikipedia, p. 15 (Grammy Award); Tinseltown, p. 15 (iHeart Radio Award); Yui Mok/ Alamy, p. 15 (BRIT Award); WFDJ_Stock, p. 15 (MTV Video Music Award); Gareth Cattermole/ Getty Images, p. 16; David M. Benett/ Getty Images, p. 17; BWM, pp. 18-19, 21; Visar Kryeziu/ AP Images, p. 20; Scott A Garfitt/ Invision/ AP Images, pp. 20-21; katatonia82, p. 23.